BLUFF YOUR WAY IN JOURNALISM

NIGEL FOSTER

RAVETTE BOOKS

Published by Ravette Books Limited
3 Glenside Estate, Star Road
Partridge Green, Horsham,
West Sussex RHl3 8RA
(0403) 710392

First printed 1988
Revised 1992

Series Editor - Anne Tauté

Cover design - Jim Wire
Printing & Binding - Cox & Wyman Ltd.
Production - Oval Projects Ltd.

The Bluffer's Guides are based on
an original idea by Peter Wolfe.

For Tara and Sacha, with love

CONTENTS

INTRODUCTION

Journalism is the ideal world for truly dedicated bluffers. Only politics, the law and advertising come close. And most of those bluffers don't even realise they're doing it.

Every year the business of journalism is flooded by would-be hopefuls, the majority of whom show a degree of competence ranging from total ineptitude to sub-human. But they don't let that stop them – and nor should you.

It doesn't matter if you can't write, can't type, and are only interested in your own opinions. It doesn't matter if, for you, the truth is something to be manipulated in order to justify your prejudices. It doesn't matter if you're as morally superior as you are ignorant, and smell like a 'before' advertisement for deodorant. If nothing else, all this will guarantee you a long and successful career working for the political press, where arrogance, stupidity and the personal hygiene of a dead skunk are taken as proof of inherent genius.

Just so long as you can bluff it out with the best of them, the moral, intellectual and material rewards will be yours.

You should not, of course, admit that you are solely interested in the money. For here is your first lesson: it doesn't matter if the bailiffs are breaking down the doors, your mortgage has been foreclosed, or your car repossessed; a journalist will never profess to be motivated by money. He or she is driven by the satisfaction of doing a good job. Of being an integral part of the democratic process. Of helping to right wrongs; of protecting the weak.

Any journalist who can say all that with a straight

face and convince other people is well on their way to becoming a success.

More importantly, he or she is probably also someone who has read this book.

GETTING THE NAME RIGHT

Ladies and gentlemen of the press (an expression that risks prosecution under the Trade Descriptions Act) are known by many titles. Many are unprintable, most professionally incorrect when used by outsiders. The one sure way to show your ignorance is to call a journalist a writer, a writer a hack, or a stringer a correspondent.

Journalist

Often shortened to 'journo'. Very much a catch-all name, this category includes reporters, leader writers and even a certain down-table sub on *The Sun*. It is also used by occasional contributors to specialist magazines when they're trying to persuade a PR agency to include them on a freebie.

Reporter

Someone in the front line, and who might know short-hand. Alternatively, one who is adept at changing the batteries in a mini-recorder when inebriated. He or she also knows how to dictate copy over a bad line to a copy-taker who is also pi-eyed but who doesn't speak English.

Reporters are usually well dressed (specially on the tabloids), carry a notebook plus pen and countless credit cards. These might even be current. The note-book is important because the editor may demand to see it if the reporter is suspected of faking a story. So most reporters become adept at writing notes that only they can understand. Except for at least one line in legible English that proves they really did hear, or see, what they claimed, and that they were in the right place at the right time to have done so. This is often known as 'authenticating a story' and much innocent amusement can be had by fixing a notebook in just such a way. Often many days after the story has appeared in print.

Reporters are also skilled at persuading an informant to give them the story even though another paper is offering more in the way of circulation, respectability or (and specially), money. There is a standard formula for doing this: it takes the form of a note shoved under a barricaded door.

Dear....

This is obviously a trying/difficult/emotional/ tragic time for you. And if you'd like to tell your story to someone who'll treat it with sympathy and understanding, please call me on my private line at the office. Certainly we can offer you protection from all other papers.'

Sadly, the average member of the public is now wise to the ways of the press. Today, any reporter chasing a shock! horror! despair! tragedy is likely to meet a demand for a four or five figure fee, and never mind the sympathy.

You should always state emphatically that newspapers didn't invent cheque book journalism, the public did. Essentially, reporters report (and always blame any inaccuracy in their copy as it finally appears on 'the office').

Scribe

A term mostly used by photographers to describe reporters. This word reflects the photographer's touching, if naïve, belief that reporters can only take dictation, preferably on parchment using a quill pen. It suggests that, at all events, the proper job for a reporter is captioning the award-winning photographs (well, they *should* have won an award) that every photographer takes on every job.

Writers

Writers are often those journos who stay in the office producing turgid 'think' pieces and editorials. These are rarely, if ever, read by the general public, particularly those that appear in the so-called 'quality' press. But they are useful in impressing government that the paper is taking its job, its rôle in society and its broader duty to the common weal, very seriously. This means that either the editor or the proprietor wants a knighthood, or that it is felt there should be some sort of balance in respect of the salacious and (if they can get away with it) scurrilous articles that really sell the paper.

Writers who produce think pieces often receive coveted invitations to accompany various ministers on fact-finding trips overseas as a reward for appearing to take the minister, the ministers' party and even politics in general, quite seriously. You must know that every journalist loves to go abroad. Not so much to broaden his or her mind, but to broaden his or her expense account.

Writers may also produce tiresomely long feature articles in the quality press. This can be a skilled process, since the writer has to disguise the fact that the piece is:

a) short on facts,

b) a rehash of a story already carried by every other newspaper, and/or has also appeared – at length – on television;

c) so obscure that less than one in ten thousand readers will understand it.

Writers may also be those lucky authors whose books regularly sell over two thousand copies in hardback, and are well regarded by the literary mafia, probably because they were all at university together and review each other's books. These writers are sometimes invited to join one of the upmarket Sundays, where they're given a flattering but quite meaningless title, like Deputy Assistant Consultant Editor. Here they're allowed to produce the occasional, self-indulgent article, but their main job is to ensure the newspaper gets first serialisation rights on their next novel.

Bluffers must know that writers like this are rarely, if ever, popular, since they can't do shorthand and vanish when it's their turn to buy the drinks.

Hacks

Originally (early 18th century), this was a word that meant someone who cheapened the entire literary profession for mere money. In other words, a term used by someone who didn't sell, about someone who did. Note that Dickens himself was accused of being a hack, and Samuel Johnson was proud of it.

Nowadays it has also come to mean the process whereby a story or article is 'hacked' into shape sometimes literally, if cut and paste are still being used. So with a certain defiant pride, many journos delight in calling themselves hacks. However, any outsider who does the same is likely to be physically assaulted.

Correspondents

Correspondents come in a great many shapes and sizes. Essentially, they're employed by a newspaper to provide news about a specific subject or from a specific place; sometimes both subject and place. Thus you have **Foreign**, **Defence** or **Parliamentary** correspondents. (Criminal correspondents do not, however, report on crime, they've merely been caught fiddling their expenses.)

Roving correspondents may be journos who are so unpopular with their colleagues – but who also have an unbreakable contract – that they have to be kept out of the office for their own sakes. Alternatively they can be relatives of Someone Important (i.e. the proprietor) who are so incompetent that they also have to be kept far, far away.

Special correspondents are either the people who have been hired for a one-off story, or the people who are sleeping with Someone Important and need a title to justify their presence on the payroll.

Our Own correspondent is often a device used to disguise the fact that the story has been taken and re-written from another source, like a news agency or rival newspaper. It can also be a person whom a reporter has met in some far-off bar, and who seems to know something about the story the reporter is after – even if it is only how to spell the name of the country they're both drinking in.

It is important to remember that most correspondents are specialists of one sort or another. Most journalists decide to specialise because it beats looking for another job. 'Why, we can't fire old Jones', says the Editor, 'He's the only person here who knows about archery', probably remembering a panic at the last Olympics. And with the delightful logic known only to editors, Old Jones finds himself dubbed Defence correspondent, when all the time he'd wanted to be a sports writer.

General reporters claim that correspondents get taken over by the subject they specialise in. This is always hotly denied by the correspondents themselves. But journalists should ask themselves when they last read an article that completely and justifiably traduced a new car. They can't all be perfect, can they?

Stringers

Stringers are invariably freelancers, and often work in the provinces. They are retained by national dailies and Sundays to provide them with local news that might warrant major coverage: 'Vicar Opens Fête' wouldn't do, but 'Vicar's Sexy Fate' might.

Stringers may be one-time reporters from the nationals who have moved to the country to escape their creditors and enemies. Stringers are also would-be journalists who are continually phoning the news editor on a national with a story that:

a) is not wanted
b) has already been carried by the news agencies, usually the previous week
c) if published, would mean prosecution under the Official Secrets Act, or for libel.

Never, ever describe yourself as stringing for a national. It's a sure way of admitting that you're out of work, or can't get a job in a metropolis.

However, you can describe yourself as stringing for a foreign newspaper so long as the newspaper doesn't have a known overseas correspondent of its own working in your own country, which sadly most of the best-known ones do.

Thus, it would be disastrous to claim to be stringing for, say, *The Washington Post*. It would be silly and suspect to claim a relationship with the *Beijing People's Daily* unless you can sing the Red Flag in Mandarin. But there are many others.

You you might consider stringing for a whole range of less well-known American newspapers – *Baltimore Sun, Hartford Courant, Fort Worth Star & Telegram*.

But not the *Christian Science Monitor*, because you might then have to behave with a certain decorum, and that might well prevent your being offered a job on a national British newspaper.

If you ever want to string for an overseas paper for real, the procedure is very simple. Just write to the paper concerned, enclosing a few sample stories you've chosen and then rewritten from that day's press. Date your letter a day or two previously, so it looks as if you really are on top of the job. Although all good overseas newspapers will use the news agencies to keep in touch, they're not going to turn down a possible good source. So you're likely to get back a polite letter, strongly non-committal, but saying yes, if you ever do get anything they print, you'll get paid for it. This is fine because your name is now somewhere in that paper's contributor's list. And if in the future some would-be employer ever bothers to check, the *Hanging Rock Courier and Express* will probably write back and confirm that you have indeed strung for them.

Cubs

Being a cub reporter was once the only way of becoming a journalist. Direct entry from university has changed things, for the worse. Today a cub reporter is someone filling in time before they break into television.

While no genuine bluffer would ever have been a cub reporter (far too much like hard work), it's important to be able to hold your own when others are reminiscing. So know that:

a) cubs, of both sexes, invariably cover the really tedious pieces and are continually bullied by other journalists

b) male cubs suffer from terminal acne

c) female cubs are ever wary of being sexually exploited or harassed, and are deeply chagrined when they're not.

Sub-editors

Subs belong to the production side of the newspaper. Their job is not actually to originate anything, but to improve – some would say ruin – a reporter's or writer's immaculate prose. Always call them "Sir" or "Ma'am".

A sub's basic job is to make filed copy fit either the available space, or the editor's own prejudices – and often both. Subs also weed out the more obvious inaccuracies and bad grammar. They can often write a bit, too.

Down-table subs mainly concern themselves with sorting out the mass of information that pours into the newspaper every day – checking it for spelling, relevance and today's date.

Page subs are, not surprisingly, responsible for putting together a complete page, and may well have two or three other subs working for them.

Stone subs are allowed to play with the actual page layout, often over the designer's unconscious body.

(Note that the word 'stone' refers to archaic printing methods and not to the sub's thinking processes.)

Some subs specialise in **features**, others in **sports**. All subs have encyclopædic memories and no newspaper could be produced without them. Even so, many reporters resent the fact that subs also call themselves journalists. This despite the fact that subs in fact belong to one of the oldest traditions in journalism, dating back to when tribal warfare broke out over whose turn it was with the chisel and tablets of stone, or how many 'ems' there are in mammoth.

Subs sometimes become **editors**. Those who do are conspicuous by their dislike of meeting the public. That, and by their obvious delight in haranguing at least one reporter a day into an early visit to the pub.

Yet all journalists are aware that subs fulfil a uniquely valuable function. It's called a Reporter's Alibi. Imagine a newspaper has run a story that has infuriated, embarrassed or even destroyed a government, a major industry, a foreign country or simply a friend of the proprietor. Say, too, that the story is either inaccurate or reveals privileged information. What is the poor reporter to do, faced with becoming a sacrificial lamb? Simple. He pulls the classic journo's bluff and blames the sub.

"God, I'm really sorry", he or she gasps contritely into the phone to their **source/contact**, "I wrote the story Just As We Agreed, but it's those bloody subs, twisted everything around and picked up the other info from God-knows-where". At this point the journo's voice begins to show real indignation: "I came near to resigning, I can tell you ... but then I realised that by staying, I can try and repair the damage with the next story I write about you/your company/your country ... so, what can you tell me?"

Note that only the feeble-minded would actually believe this bluff. No matter: it's face-saving time, and the source or contact can carry on enjoying the reporter's lavish hospitality for a long time to come.

The difference between a **source** and a **contact** is simple. A contact is, like as not, official and certainly will not be secret; whereas a source is unofficial and often clandestine. At least, so the journalist par excellence would have his editor believe. This disguises the fact that the source isn't actually human, but in part composed of the cuttings library and in part fertile imagination. This allows you to file some massive expense claims for entertainment.

However, subs are, by and large, not to be messed with. Don't try to bluff them with your brilliance and expertise. Reverse it:

* Make yourself out to be totally insignificant, but hint at a family relationship with the proprietor.

* Admire the subs and their work in an awe-struck sort of way.

* Go on record as realising that you're not good enough to be a sub – which is why you're forced to endure the drudgery of reporting.

Never forget, a sub can turn your definite 'page one splash' into a three-line item buried in the classifieds. Remember also that subs stick together. Insult one and you insult the lot; and subs never forget. They also attack en masse, rather like ants. Reporters delight in telling horror stories about Subs They Have Known. But true friendships are rare.

Magazine Journalists

These are journalists who work on:

a) the supplements that come free with Sunday news-papers and have the occasional editorial feature sandwiched between wonderful glossy ads, and

b) a variety of genuine magazines, many of which specialise in something that logic (but not public taste) suggests is infantile or irrelevant.

Newspaper magazine journalists are often arrogant, working as they do with colour and to a deadline fully six weeks – sometimes months – ahead. Or dealing with superb photographs of beggars in Calcutta or the newest hot news from California (illustrated naturally, by the trendiest young artist to come out of the Royal College of Art this year) on reducing body fat.

Magazine magazine journalists often spend many a long and weary hour wondering why they appear doomed to spend the rest of their days writing about fish, fashion or the inconsequential musings of a minor celebrity, and why straight news reporters won't take them seriously. The answer to the former is someone has to do it; to the latter, that newspaper journos have an instinctive mistrust of anyone who doesn't possess a similarly low boredom threshold.

Magazine journalists are also often freelance, rarely professionally trained, and the objects of envy of other journalists who suspect with some truth that:

- their expense accounts are higher
- their foreign trips more frequent
- their lunches longer and more liquid.

Dealing with magazine journalists should pose little or no problem for the experienced. Refer, fleetingly, to your time on *Paris Match* and *Life Magazine*. Drop hints about some pretty exciting, and dangerous, assignments you've had. This will drive them quietly wild since, while all magazine journalists accept that the magazines must feature all those 'lifestyle' articles (more crucial than macho photo-journalism); and while all magazine journos also accept that it's the ads that are really important (certainly as far as most of the readers are concerned); all magazine journalists are deeply ashamed of both facts..

As for the odd journalist who really does enjoy producing articles like *Is Smoked Salmon Good For The Skin?*, he or she can be bluffed by your claim to have known Andy Warhol. Or the promise of a secret recipe for bouillabaisse.

Journalists who work on Sunday **tabloid magazines** are quite shameless, but can be bluffed by your claim to be the only journalist to have seen Elton John without his hat, or hair.

Photographers

Photographers are also known as 'phots', 'snappers' or 'animals'. This last is as much because they like travelling in packs, as it is a reflection on their personal habits. Phots only care about the picture and pleasing the **Photo Editor** a one-time news phot himself, but now fully housetrained. You should be able to recount, ruefully, being knocked to the ground by a phot because you came between him and his subject. (Tourists in Canada have similar problems when getting between a mother bear and her cubs. On balance, the bear is marginally easier to outwit – and won't insist on you buying it drinks afterwards.)

Never pretend to know anything about news photography. You'll be talking to people who can instinctively set the right speed, the right aperture, light a cigarette, scream out 'Over 'ere, luv', raise the camera to their eye and take the shot in under one second.

Never refer to a phot as a photo-journalist, as this implies the ability to write a bit or to produce something almost artistic – both of which the real news phot will find embarrassing. The term is only used by:

- writers who know just enough to take the lense cap off and check that the camera is loaded

- academics who teach media courses

- studio or fashion photographers who fancy themselves as a bit special, and have conned some unsuspecting publisher into fronting the money for a lavish-looking book that will be featured in one of the Sunday magazines, thereafter selling all of twenty-five copies.

In the world of news photography, war photographers are regarded as being the professional's professional. It is more than acceptable for the journalist to bemoan the death of good news photography, pointing out how well it's survived in Europe – particularly in

France, Germany and Italy. This goes over well with any phot you may be talking to (or rather, buying drinks for). You could wonder if perhaps this sanitization of the Sunday magazines hasn't been at the request of the advertisers, who dislike seeing their ads next to a shot of something or someone that's painfully real.

You might mention cynically that the Sunday magazines must provide infinitely more rewarding 'freebies' than when Bert Hardy or Don McCullin were at their height. Then hasten to add that you're not, of course, accusing anyone in particular. After a few minutes, the phot should start telling you exactly which editors and sub-editors are getting back-handers from advertisers. For along with advertising reps, phots know all the gossip, all the scandal.

As with subs, the best way of bluffing them is to denigrate yourself. Agree that one picture is worth a thousand words, and remember that often, it is.

Freelancers

As actors 'rest' between jobs, so too will journalists often freelance. This has been known to last for some years. However, many publications rely heavily on genuine freelancers, those who do get paid (albeit a pittance) because they:

a) cringe a lot
b) can easily be let go.

The general rule is that the louder freelancers claim to be enjoying the life, the more desperately they're seeking a permanent job.

KNOW YOUR COLLEAGUES

Most journalists fall into a few distinct types. Given that your aim may be to:
  a) impress them or
  b) terrify them
you should learn to identify which type another journalist belongs to, and to handle that type successfully.

1. Solid Professional

Content to remain a sub or reporter for ever. Probably learnt his or her trade on a terribly respectable provincial newspaper. Does fluent shorthand. Dresses in a neat and far from gaudy fashion. Was once a strong Union supporter.

Impressed by: faster shorthand speeds and a dislike of graduate trainees.

Terrified by: natural ability to write and/or natural charm.

2. Hot Shot Graduate

Really biding their time until the right television spot turns up. Probably went to Oxbridge, where she/he became known for frightfully witty pieces in the university paper. Does no shorthand, but did meet the proprietor's son/daughter at university, who is now the Hot Shot's best friend/lover.

Impressed by: crime reporters.

Terrified by: classics scholars and spots.

3. **Working Class Brutal**

Sometimes a natural writer, always a natural bully. Determined to be editor within two years. Excellent technical skills.

Impressed by: genuine gourmets and anyone apparently tougher than they are.

Terrified by: someone discovering that they are really middle class.

4. **Slinky Fragrant**

The female of the species and far deadlier than the male. Is often reticent about how she came to get her job. Colleagues strongly suspect it's because she's the editor's mistress. Truth is, the editor only wishes she was.

Impressed by: people who realise she does have a brain.

Terrified by: missing any fashionable party.

5. **Supertrend**

Either male or female, sometimes fashionably both. Dresses for impact, not for comfort. Claims to be in touch with all the latest fads, gossip and "what the kids really feel, right?"

Often employed in desperation by an editor facing falling circulation. Incapable of doing shorthand or even taking accurate notes. Also found in television where desperate enthusiasm is deemed to compensate for any lack of talent.

Impressed by: anyone who has slept with someone more fashionable, or influential, than they have.

Terrified by: someone discovering they are nearly, or over, thirty.

6. Shabbier-Than-Thou

Usually male, this superannuated hippy wears as motley a collection of clothes as you could find this side of Skid Row. And often as dirty. Is widely regarded by colleagues as being a creative genius and relatively harmless. How wrong they are, for this animal bites. He is totally egocentric and ruthless, wears the hippytrippy camouflage all the better to steal your career, your reputation, and probably your lover. Is often seen with a Slinky Fragrant – who can recognise a fellow survivor when she sees one.

Terrified by: being forced to wear clean, matching socks.

Impressed by: anyone more ruthless than himself.

7. Ms Do-It-My-Way

A female who's often become a journalist via the production side, or administration, or because she knows all about the proprietor's most secret perversion. Invariably has an esoteric and quite useless degree. Hides a lack of talent behind a no-nonsense air of authority. When challenged, first becomes abusive and then saccharine sweet. Is often deeply interested in sex. Sex does not appear to return the interest.

Impressed by: anyone reasonably important who appears to take her seriously. Often found on late night chat shows for this reason.

Terrified by: anyone reasonably important who doesn't take her seriously.

Whatever type, colleagues really do matter, more so than anyone else, for:
– they can help you find a job
– they can help you keep it
– they can lend you money.

Since your colleagues may be as adept at bluffing as you are, don't expect outright success. There are two golden rules, and if you follow them you'll earn their undying respect. At least until, you move to a new paper:

1. Never appear to believe your own bluffs.
2. Always keep a sense of humour.

This effectively marks you as a rogue as opposed to a sociopath. Since most sociopaths are themselves excellent bluffers, no-one will ever know the truth about you. Which is what bluffing is really all about.

By These Signs Shall Ye Know Them

A good journalist should be able to tell if another journalist is from:

- a **tabloid** or
- a **broadsheet**

without being introduced. Sometimes it's also possible to know whether they are a general reporter or a specialist.

Broadly speaking, tabloid journalists are far smarter in appearance. Whether they're better dressed is a moot point and depends upon your point of view.

Tabloid

Male tabloid journalists tend to look like successful time-share salesmen. Occasionally you will meet one who affects a crumpled suit, scuffed suede shoes, woolly cardigan, battered trilby and dirty raincoat. This man is treated with reverential contempt by his colleagues – he's usually in his late fifties, and is seen as being something of a dinosaur. HE IS TO BE AVOIDED AT ALL COSTS, for he's forgotten more about bluffing than you'll ever know, and will steal a story from you as easily as a politician will lie on camera.

The pockets of a male tabloid journo's clothes, should you ever have the opportunity to go through them, will probably reveal:

- the usual collection of credit cards
- various ID cards
- one pager and one mini-recorder, in working order, and possibly a lapel microphone disguised as a Rotary pin
- various business cards, some of which may even be in his own name
- a mouthspray
- nicotine gum

26

- the business card of a massage parlour (visited for purely for professional reasons)
- coded address book
- forged memo from the editor praising his last story
- assorted cuttings
- his expense claim, i.e. a collection of blank receipts.

Add to this loose change, penknives, pens, etc., and you can understand how hard it is to remain wrinkle free.

Female tabloid journos carry much the same, often in handbags the size of a small (but expensive) suitcase. Their massage parlour card is for an expensive, all-female retreat, and clippings are replaced by a permanently unposted letter to an ex-boyfriend or husband.

Broadsheet

Male broadsheet journos affect either a Patrician or an Intellectual look which could in many cases benefit from being taken to the dry-cleaners.

For a broadsheet male journo (*Genus Intellectualis*) the look is: shapeless sports jacket, baggy cords, stained suede shoes, coloured shirt and no tie.

His pockets will show:

- a broken pager
- a notebook covered in coffee stains
- one out-of-date credit card
- one crumpled business card, dating from his last job
- a press ID card covered in teeth marks

- a poetry paperback written by an obscure Armenian and translated into French
- his home and office phone numbers written on the back of his expense claim
- scraps of paper covered in hieroglyphics which represent the story he's currently working on
- a massage parlour business card (he suffers from a bad back).

The broadsheet male journo (*Genus Patricianus*) wears: a three-piece suit, wool, never lightweight and always dark, a striped shirt, a striped tie that denotes membership of something, even if it's only a local video club, and Oxford shoes, usually black.

While obviously expensive, his clothes will never be well pressed. His pockets will contain much the same as his intellectual colleague – although the massage parlour might be replaced by a someone who offers colonic irrigation.

However, broadsheet journos (male) can also belong to the genus *Solidus Professionalis*, usually those who went to grammar school before Oxbridge. They are allowed to wear two-piece suits, preferably with an MCC tie.

Be aware that just as the clothes change, so do the physical types. Thus tabloid journos tend to be short to medium height, while broadsheet (*Patricianus*) are often tall, lean and questing in their youth; well padded and avuncular in middle age.

Genus Solidus Professionalis is usually of medium height and worries about keeping fit.

Female broadsheet journos are harder to define. What can be said is that *Genus Intellectualis* wears jeans in her youth, graduates to the Oxfam shop later on, and has difficulty with shaving her armpits; while whatever the female *Patricianus* wears it's essentially a variation of twin-set-and-pearls.

Female tabloid journalists dress with extreme aggression, except the very good ones, who try to look like a secretary (albeit one who can afford to spend several hundred pounds on a new bag).

The point behind all journalists' dressing (other than an intense tribal instinct) is they dress in accordance with the people they meet. So it is that **business** journos either look like bankers or insurance salesmen. **Showbiz** reporters look like managers and agents, sometimes like showbiz stars themselves. **Court** reporters (the ones who officially report on the Royal Family) try to look as if they come out of the very top drawer. Even down to wearing Old Etonian ties.

Crime reporters may resemble the thugs they write about, but mostly they dress, sound and look like plain-clothes policemen. Which is useful in trying to bluff an exclusive story from a reluctant witness.

From this short example, you will realise that not only do clothes make the man – they make the entire job.

KNOW WHO REALLY MATTERS

Proprietors

These come in basically two manifestations: those who know about journalism and newspapers, and those who don't.

Both are equally devoted to making money. Both are almost impossible to bluff – the former because they know far more than you do; and the latter because they probably won't even notice you. For it is a well-known fact that a proprietor's egotism increases in inverse proportion to the amount he knows about the business.

Proprietors Who Know are usually surrounded by equally bright individuals. The only bluff here is to pretend that you're not in the least bit awed by them. No-one will believe you, but you'll get full marks for trying.

Proprietors Who Don't Know are usually surrounded by a coterie of advisers resembling a medieval court, and one which Lucretia Borgia would have loved (see chief flunkies).

The proprietor matters most of all. After that, members of his family are vital. (Proprietors are invariably male, except in America where by law a certain percentage have to be female, black, and homosexual.)

Chief Flunkies

Not all proprietors have a chief flunky, but when he is there, he can be very dangerous indeed. Chief flunkies don't appear to have any proper function. However to dismiss them on these grounds would be to show your basic inexperience. Simply put, chief flunkies exist because the proprietor wants them to. He is paying them at least five times their market worth; but in so doing he's buying loyalty. For all chief flunkies are bright enough to know how incredibly lucky they are to have such a well-paid job, and will do anything to keep it. Anything at all.

So Proprietors use chief flunkies to:

- do all those unpleasant jobs that other staff refuse to do, like sack the longest-serving and best journalist on the paper because he/she's upset the proprietor's wife
- tell the proprietor at frequent intervals how brilliant he is
- silence any opposition to the proprietor's plans at meetings
- arrange for the proprietor's biography to be written by a totally unbiased author. Then take the blame when the world complains, or laughs, at how biased the biography actually is. (Sometimes the chief flunky undertakes this arduous task himself.)

Chief flunkies are always men: women have too great a sense of the absurd. In handling them remember that, more than anyone else except the proprietor, they know how vulnerable their position is. They know that if fired, they'd be lucky to end up running a sheep-dip in the Falklands. So you have to convince a chief flunky that you are someone he can count on while making sure never to allow him to embroil you in the proprietor's more harebrained schemes. Don't ever think that you can sidestep the chief flunky by earning the proprietor's respect and admiration. Chief flunkies are only ever worried or affected by other flunkies; they know that come the crunch, the proprietor will fire you rather than his favourite back-scratcher.

In dealing with flunkies two distinct types of bluff are possible:

- that you know Something about them which would infuriate the proprietor, so they better be nice to you

- that you really do regard them as being highly intelligent executives and worth every penny they're being paid.

Editors

Editors are a lonely lot, characterised by the belief that they are, individually, the best writers/journalists in the world. Always remember that editors, more than anyone else, live in fear of losing their jobs for where else can they go? Ideally, you should avoid editors at all costs. But if you do find yourself in day-to-day contact with them, there are two bluffs worth considering:

1. that you're capable of far greater things than you've been given the chance to produce (dangerous one this, since you will invariably be given the chance one day)

2. that you know Something not very nice about the proprietor.

News Editors

This hapless breed control the newsroom and are, not surprisingly, responsible to the Editor for the news content of the paper. There's little point in trying to bluff them more than once, and then only in attempting to get the 'page one splash'. News editors don't really care if you're lying through your teeth, so long as the story reads well and will hold up for twenty four hours.

Features Editors

These live a more leisurely existence than News Editors, since they usually have a fraction longer to produce a single feature. The bluff here is to get to work for them in the first instance. This you do by:

- claiming to have the greatest contacts in the world

- producing a very impressive set of samples (taking from one source is plagiarism, from several it's research)

- intimating a sojourn at a very good school – in which case you may not need samples, nor indeed the ability to write as the subs will do it for you. But you will need a vaguely aristocratic sounding name, so invent one. Everyone else seems to.

This should, with luck, result in at least a freelance commission. Make sure it involves travelling. That way, you merely supply hard facts via fax, telex or satellite telephone for the subs to write up, claiming that you're strike bound in some far-off airport.

Just so long as the facts you supply are interesting, you'll be able to hide the fact that you can't string two words together for many, many productive years.

City Editors

Bear in mind that these people spend most of their time dealing with bankers, stockbrokers, city investors, etc. They are therefore not dumb and are used to dealing with all sorts of con-persons. If you're trying to get a job on a City Desk, it's not a good idea to say:

* "Naturally, I'll pass any good tips along to you." (The City Editor makes a living out of tips he gets direct – how else could he afford that Rolls-Royce?)

* "I see my job as tracking down and exposing the real City villains." (Do that, and shortly there would be precious little City left. Ergo, nothing to write about. Ergo you'd all be out of a job.)

However, you might try:

* "I see the job more as a responsibility really, to help keep the wheels of finance moving smoothly... and very occasionally, to help expose those who threaten the market's stability." Notice here that you've said nothing about crooks and dishonesty.

You could, on that basis, expose the bumbling but honest whistleblower with evidence of a major stock fraud as being guilty of slander, libel, defamation and generally 'economical' with the truth. Your exposures wouldn't be true, of course, but that's business. You will have established yourself as a potential and willing stooge. Later, you can write a book that really does expose the City and retire early.

Sports Editors

These are responsible for the second most important element in a newspaper - the sports pages. The first important element is the headline on page one and/or the girl on page three.

All journalists love to see themselves as being *the* expert on a given subject. Sports editors are like this, but even more so. If you want to get on the right side of a sports editor, and you've absolutely no sporting background yourself, simply invent one. Choose a sport no-one knows very much about and claim either to have been one of the leading players (before injury forced your premature retirement) or the person who really put that sport on the map. And hope that no-one asks which map.

Sports you might think about are:

a) synchronised swimming (women as participants; men having trained the world champions);

b) sumo wrestling (don't pretend to have practised this, unless you're an anorexic-looking eighteen stones. Just claim to have been the person who brought the sport to the West);

c) lacrosse, real lacrosse that is, the Canadian national game and one that's just as vicious as it was when played by Indians using a human head.

The point is that not only sports journalists but all journalists find it hard to respect someone who is not an expert on something. Nor does the subject need to have anything whatsoever to do with your paid job. This may be because journalism attracts people who used to collect train numbers in their youth and only feel at home with someone who's been similarly addicted.

So if you're one of those strange individuals who actually enjoys your job and needs no other stimulation, hide the fact. Learn to enjoy collecting strange objects. Become an expert (or pretend to be one). You will thus become 'sound', and as such, employable.

Lawyers

As we all know, lawyers have the natural right to earn a good living from the law in any way they can, and everyone else has a natural obligation to help them do so. This means that both journalism, and journalists individually, are as bedevilled by lawyers as any other business. Probably more so, since lawyers are often required to 'sign off' every edition. If the newspaper carries libel insurance, the 'signing off' by the lawyer effectively states that there's nothing libellous or defamatory present, or if there is, that it's not about anyone who's likely to sue; or if they do, they won't win, or if they win, they won't get all that much; or if they get a great deal, most of it will go on lawyers' fees anyway.

This is known as 'preserving one's legal options'.

There are however, a few lawyers who see their first duty as being to the journalist, and who will fight to the death to get a contentious piece printed. But most delight not only in killing a story stone dead, but also in rewriting it, thus proving that they're as brilliant a journalist as they are lawyer. They also see their first duty as proving how indispensable they are, and tend to find something libellous or defamatory in almost everything. But as it's the editor who carries the can if anything does go wrong, lawyers tend to be listened to.

(It should also be said that the importance and self-importance of lawyers within journalism is mostly because of the ludicrous and contradictory libel laws. However, since only lawyers could draft new ones which would cut down their earning power, the situation is not likely to change.)

The best way of showing how to bluff lawyers is with a scenario.

You have spent months producing a superbly written, well researched and documented article (one that is actually true), proving that a leading politician is:

a) a transvestite
b) working for the CIA.

This is not quite enough to force him, or her, to be stripped of their peerage and Harrods' credit card, perhaps, but you can also prove that the politician despises animals (especially cute, furry ones), Bobby Charlton, Mother Theresa, the Royal Navy and The Queen Mother. All of which is quite enough to bring down the government; may even result in being interviewed by David Frost.

Your editor insists the lawyers see it first. By the time they've finished with it, you've written a piece praising the politician for his or her:

a) interest in minority groups
b) respect for the sporting amateur
c) concern for the Third World
d) support for defence
e) reverence for tradition.

Where did you go wrong? The wise could tell you that with lawyers, the best defence is attack. You should have known what the lawyers would do and forestalled them.

You could, for example, have claimed with complete conviction that most if not all your comments had already appeared in print, and cited totally fictitious instances. (The defence in law here would be that if the politician hadn't sued before, why should he do so now?)

You could also intimate that you have, in fact, been put up to writing the piece by the Prime Minister's office, and that it has the backing of all the most senior mandarins in the civil service. Not to mention the RSPCA, Ministry of Defence and the Football Association. If lawyers love one thing besides themselves and occasionally, each other, it's the establishment.

Finally, you can claim that the proprietor is very keen to see your article printed (make sure it's at a time when he's out of the country and can't be reached) and that *The Sun* is on to the same story. Point out gently that it's the lawyers' job, after all, to please the proprietor as much as the insurance company.

Occasionally you'll find a lawyer who will accept none of your arguments; who will demand proof that similar allegations have been made before; who will want a meeting with Someone from the PM's Office;

who will insist in speaking personally to the proprietor. If that happens, you have only one course left. Discredit the lawyer.

Have a colleague spread the rumour that he/she is a close business colleague of the politician in question. With any luck, the lawyer will be removed and replaced by a more malleable junior. If all else fails, you can always try blackmailing the editor by threatening to resign. It won't do any good, but any dedicated journalist should threaten to resign at least once a week. It makes it look as if you really do care.

Some lawyers might respond to threats of physical violence, i.e. they'll back down. Unless they've spent some time in criminal practice, in which case they'll make a brief phone call and you'll be invited to meet a few of their ex-clients, probably in a dark alley down by the river. It would be a little silly to accept such an invitation. You might catch a cold.

Agony Aunts

By and large, Agony Aunts are the acceptable face of tabloid journalism, inasmuch as they care, often quite dreadfully, about their jobs. As well they might, since advice columns are one of the best-read parts of the newspaper, by men and women alike. Particularly those advice columns that somehow manage to print all the naughty bits.

You're unlikely to have all that much to do with Agony Aunts, unless you've got plans of becoming one yourself. Either way, it is worth knowing that **AA**s fall into one of several categories:

1. The Enthusiastically Understanding

Could find a silver lining in a hurricane that laid waste New York. Sample line in chat: "Look, love, I know how worried you might be at catching HIV – but really, it's quite normal, nothing to be ashamed of. Think of it as being a marvellous opportunity to meet new people and for spiritual growth."

Can be bluffed by admitting, tearfully, that your father had lesbian tendencies.

2. The Practical Heart of Gold

Has the best line in sexy problems. Sample line in chat: "Well, you have been a little slut, haven't you? I'm not surprised your husband objected to you making love to his teammates on the coach. But the fact that he left you by an emergency telephone on the motorway does show he still cares ..."

Can be bluffed by admitting, with a rueful grin, that you've discovered love is as important as sex.

3. The Determinedly Modern

Usually found in desperately trendy women's magazines. Sample line in chat: "No, there's nothing wrong with falling in love with your daughter's boyfriend the age gap shouldn't make any difference, but do be careful how you tell your wife."

Can be bluffed by admitting, bravely, how ashamed you are at not being bisexual.

It's worthwhile getting Agony Aunts on your side

since they're often the only journalists whom the proprietor's wife wants to meet.

Accountants

Every journalist attempts to bluff the accountants whenever he or she puts in their expense claim.

Remember that accountants never believe expense claims – suspecting, with some justification, that journalists are incapable of being honest about them.

The lesson is to bluff on a grand scale.

A trip to the Middle East should result in an expense claim not just for hiring camels, but also for hiring an entire Bedouin tribe as guides and guards, backed up by suitable receipts scrawled in bad Arabic (these can be obtained at most Middle Eastern airports for a small fee).

A trip to New York should result in an expense claim for entertaining several Mafia godfathers. Or Gore Vidal.

Even a trip to Birmingham could result in a hefty claim for being mugged repeatedly while driving round the Bull Ring.

And in London, a drink bought for a colleague turns into dinner with a source at Bibendum.

Readers

These are the people you should know how to bluff most of all. The less sure you are of your facts, the more authoritative you should become. This will prevent most readers from challenging you via a nasty letter to the editor. Those that do will probably be simply insulting.

Conversely, you can sometimes appear to be a little unsure about something that you know, and can prove to be untrue. Then, when the angry letters arrive to denounce you, quietly produce your proof – either in the form of another article, or as a reply to the letters. This will make any other reader think twice before challenging you again, as well as impressing your colleagues who (mostly) love seeing a reader properly squelched.

Always suggest you know a good deal more than you're actually telling, even if you know a good deal less. This helps establish you as having both integrity and a suitable professional caution.

Make even the most trivial piece of information sound important. This helps convince the reader that they were right to buy that particular newspaper in the first place, while not demanding too much from them in the way of critical analysis.

Sadly it has to be admitted that you need the readers far more than they need you, a fact of life which most journalists try to overcome by bluffing the public into believing how necessary journalists are.

Assorted Lowlife

Salespeople (display and classified) have the unfortunate habit of saying that it's their work that pays your salary. This is partly true. When you run across them try to appear genuinely interested in what they do.

Say you'd be happy to see a story killed to make
way for a last-minute ad. This will win them to your
side, which is important because salespeople know all
the gossip. Quite why this should be so, no-one
knows. But they do, and it's pretty accurate, too.

Marketing people are those who aren't extrovert
enough to make it selling advertising space. Their
latest marketing plan invariably proves as
indigestible as the last. Other people have sex.
Marketing people have research.

Advertising people talk of campaigns that will 'raise
reader awareness by high profiling the product's
acceptable lifestyle image'. In other words, tell the
readers that they like reading your newspaper.
Which, it might be assumed, they know anyway.
  Advertising people are arrogant in the extreme but
can be bluffed into a state of manic fury (particularly
the creatives) by pointing out that everything they do
is second-hand anyway. It might not be, but every ad
person lives in mortal fear that they've reproduced
someone else's ideas without realising it. Or that,
having knowingly done so, they're about to be exposed
as lacking real creativity.

You will have noticed that we have not mentioned
journalists who become gossip columnists. In this we
have obeyed the First Law of Survival: never attack
anyone who can get you back.

KNOW WHAT HARDLY MATTERS

PROs

Every good journalist has to know how the game of
bluff is played with those who are specially designated
to 'handle' the press. They are variously called Press
Officers, Public Relations Officers or Press Agents.
Their whole aim in life is to try and ensure that the
press is given all the information and help it needs in
order to print stories that are:

- accurate
- fair
- free of prejudice.

This of course explains why, in trying to control a
situation that threatens to get out of control (i.e. the
truth is about to come out), PROs will claim:

a) nothing happened

b) if it did, we don't know anything about it

c) if you print a word, that's the last exclusive you'll
   ever get from us.

On the other hand, the journalist will attempt to bluff
PROs that:

a) he/she knows far more than they do

b) every other paper is going to be carrying the story

c) given an exclusive, he/she will make sure the story
   is sympathetic.

The thing to remember is that the game is played within known limits. PROs have a (largely) thankless job to do; and the least you can do is let them buy you lunch every now and then.

The situation changes when the Press Officer, or whoever, is trying to get a story into the papers, rather than keep one out. If working for business or industry, they'll buy you lunch, or even fly you to exotic locations, the better to view the latest in plastic drainage pipe.

There are certain stock phrases that cover the **release of information** to the press:

Off the record (sadly over-used, now happily going out of style) – "I'll tell you what you want to know on the understanding you won't print it." In real terms, the journalist waits about two weeks, then prints the story. Often used by people who know they've been found out, or think that if they admit to something 'off the record' it will stop the journalist publishing. It doesn't.

Not for publication – Used to cover confidential information that can't be printed, but explains why the government or whomever is behaving so oddly.

Embargoed – Information that can't be used until such and such a date. Usually put on press releases as it makes the PRO feel important to think that he/she is controlling the news; not realising that ninety-nine per cent of all press releases are junked anyway.

Non-attributable – "Use this, but don't even dare suggest that someone official told you."

Unattributable – "Use this, but don't dare suggest that I told you."

Confidential source – Official spokesperson.

Unofficial source – Conversation overhead in a bar.

Sources close to – The person him or herself.

Overall, the main bluff journalists must watch out for is: "Don't print this and I'll make it up to you later." They never do.

Press Conferences

These are formal occasions at which journalists can show off their new clothes to each other. Often enlivened by television journalists asking such incisive questions as: "How do you feel now that your family has been eaten by crocodiles?" Or "Will bankruptcy make much difference to your life?"

Press Receptions

Reflecting the eternal optimism (some would say stupidity) of human beings, press receptions are held in the belief that if you're nice to journalists, give them something to eat and a lot to drink, they'll be nice to you in return.

As PROs continually discover, the only journalists who are nice in return are the ones who work for not-very-important newspapers.

The golden rule at press receptions is to appear more important than you really are. Do not be seen carrying any of the enormous amounts of bumf given out. Ask for it to be sent round to your office as you have to go somewhere else afterwards – like a front-line a few thousand miles away.

Facilities

Often known as trips, sometimes as freebies, these are specially arranged visits to a factory, military exercise, war zone, testing ground or whatever. Give the impression of knowing what's going on; an admission of ignorance on your part may win you marks for honesty and candour, but it won't get you invited back.

The Press Complaints Commission

The quaint organisation that is theoretially responsible for upholding journalistic standards. It appears to be obsessed with tabloid excesses, but this could be because a number of tabloid editors have been co-opted onto it. The Commission is meant to be (self)regulatory, which means it displays a willingness to apologise at the drop of any scoop that seriously embarrasses the establishment.

There is little or no need to bluff the PCC. Do what everyone else does: ignore it and it soons goes away.

KNOW YOUR GOSSIP

Whenever journalists gather together after a hard day serving the public and defending liberty, relaxing with a little crochet work, perhaps, sipping the dryest of sherries from delicate crystal, or biting the heads from live doves, the talk often gently turns to Who is doing What and to Whom. You might be a superb writer, but unless you give good gossip you'll have failed as a would-be journalist.

Like drinking and paranoia, gossip goes with the job. However, you must be aware of certain incontrovertible facts: the greater the scandal, the more it will embarrass its subject, and the greater the influence he or she has over your career, the sooner they will know what you have said about them.

Imagine, you have the most delicious story about your editor, an affair with the proprietors' wife, a rent-boy and – if you're working for a Sunday tabloid – at least one nervous breakdown affecting said individual following an interview with Scotland Yard. You tell it, superbly, to your colleagues in the pub one night. You would swear that no-one left the table. Yet within minutes of finishing, you're called to the telephone and suspended for a week. Or, if your story-telling took place at lunch time, you arrive back in the office, with your colleagues, to find a message on your screen telling you to clear your desk.

How on earth did the editor find out? Probably from one of the bar staff. Or a friend with a mobile phone. On the other hand, part of an editors' survival kit lies in always knowing exactly what's being said about him, or her, which often amounts to telepathy.

The golden rules for how to give good gossip and hold your job are :

1. Never tell more than one person at a time.

2. Remember that walls probably do have ears (bug-shaped) so never gossip in the office.

3. Once a story that you started is going the rounds, disclaim all responsibility for it. If it's repeated back to you, act as if you never heard it.

4. Never tell a juicy piece of factual and damaging gossip to anyone unless you're assured of something equally damaging and dangerous in return.

Of course, it's not always easy to know if this will happen. This explains why many journos spend many hours talking eliptically to each other, not wanting to be the first to begin, often confining themselves to gossip that was old when Caxton was a printer's devil.

Naturally, human nature being what it is, sometimes the urge to tell becomes overwhelming. After all, an overwhelming urge to find out and tell is why most people become journalists in the first place.

When this happens, and assuming you don't have a close friend you would trust with your life, there is only one recourse: tell it to a freelancer without friends in high places.

Then repeat it to a colleague, claiming the freelancer as the prime source. This way, the freelancer will be blamed. It is a matter of some pride within journalism that a freelancer's word is never, ever taken before that of a staffer. But don't feel too badly; they might gain considerably kudos as someone who gives good gossip. They might even be offered a permanent job.

At some time, people will begin to gossip about you.

Sometimes this gossip will be both true and damaging. (If you haven't something secret and even shameful in your life, you shouldn't be a journalist: how can you begin to understand the foibles of others without a few of your own?)

Never hope to ignore gossip about yourself. As any good journalist will confirm, silence suggests guilt. Many a career shattering story has been written on that very basis. So come out fighting – and deny everything, thrice.

Finally, never gossip to anyone markedly senior to yourself. They may just begin to wonder what you're saying about them.

Know Your Newspapers

All journalists like to talk about the opposition. Admiringly if they're thinking of a career move. Disparagingly if they think they're in line for a raise. Enthusiasts should also be able to name-drop a few less well-known newspapers, and with them the names of journalists who sound as if they work there as in "old Chet Collins who wrote that great piece on cocaine smuggling for the *Miami Herald*".

You can say this secure in the knowledge that:

a) the *Miami Herald* is bound to have carried at least a hundred articles about cocaine smuggling over the past year;

b) if by a chance in a million one of your audience actually knows the *Miami Herald* and flatly denies Chet Collins ever worked there, you can always say:

"Hey, you're right, I meant the *Tampa Bay Express.*"

So here, are a few suggestions:

Newspaper	Journalist	Story
Cleveland Plain Dealer	Tina Amalfi	Mafia-owned funeral parlour
L.A. Times	Sallee Marks	Friendly crystals
Toronto Star	Gordo Viczak	Rabid chipmunks
Straits Times (S'pore)	Jenny Tan	20 ways to eat a durian
Kaleej Times (Dubai)	Saeed Khassar	'What Gulf War?'

The papers must be real; the people and stories must sound real. But watch out for the person who suddenly remembers the same article and knows the journo who you claim wrote it. Either you've been rumbled, or you're talking to a complete drongo.

Brief History

Most journalists affect to know nothing about the history of their profession. Most journalists don't even like to admit they belong to a profession. They spend too much time covering the sins and crimes of doctors, lawyers, accountants and spies to be impressed by 'the professions'. Yet there comes a point in many journalists' careers when they become experts on the history and traditions of journalism, such as:

- when they've finally been passed over for promotion and are beginning to assume the rôle of Grand Old Man/Woman who's loved by all

- when, as editors, it's the only way they can hope to achieve some level of dominance over the crass new proprietor.

It's worth noting that while journalists do despise the professions, they also pride themselves on being professional – defined as the ability to write ten paragraphs on any subject in the world in ten minutes flat. That, and the ability to make up quotes which sound so authentic as to fool the person supposed to have said them.

You should cultivate a certain cynical, even outré, knowledge of the history of the business. Use this when losing an argument with established journos, or when trying to impress the new proprietor. You might, for example:

1. Refer to Eve as the first journalist who made the fatal error of blindly trusting her source (snake) and closest colleague (Adam). As a result she upset the Great Proprietor, and was banished from the News Room.

2. Explain that Homer was the first War Correspondent. And no-one complained that he was blind and reported battles that he'd been nowhere near. Nor that he said it in verse.

3. Prove that Gaius Petronius Arbiter was the first gossip columnist (the Satyricon). Petronius chose suicide rather than retraction following a fearless

52

exposé of Nero's Rome. The chances of Nigel Dempster doing something similar are, sadly, slight.

4. Confirm that yes, the first real newspapers were tabloids, but the word itself means a drug in a compressed form. Originally scurrilous sheets of gossip, printed on cheap yellow paper (hence Yellow Press), today's tabs are merely carrying on a long and noble tradition. This will infuriate any journalist from the 'quality' press who may be listening, which is no bad thing to do once in a while.

5. Claim that Stanley actually intended to say: 'Dr Livingstone, I presume you do have an answer to these charges of taking part in local fertility rites?' but was cut short by the appearance of Livingstone's press agent, clutching an exclusive contract with *The Glasgow Herald.*

The point is to demonstrate both your total disregard for silly tradition and devotion to the past by appearing to be both knowledgeable and contentious. This will establish you as Someone To Be Reckoned With in other journalists' eyes and may bring you interesting commissions.

Of course it may just mean that someone will buy you a drink to shut you up. Either way you've gained a little.

BLUFF YOUR WAY ON TO THE FRONT PAGE

Every journalist aspires to having the page one splash especially if it's with an exclusive story. There's no real fun in having your by-line under the same story that every other paper has run. Unfortunately, it's not easy. Competition is fierce, and really good stories don't happen every day. This is where the champion journalist comes into his or her own, with a largely bogus story that you've bluffed people into confirming, and the editor into believing. (Editors have to believe that any story they print is at least partly true. That way they can answer charges of false reporting with a clear conscience.)

Whatever you choose, decide on your headline and thence your story. (There's nothing strange in this: at least one Sunday tabloid features editor thinks first of the head, then the layout before deciding on the story.) Of course, when the story does break the real headline will be written by a sub. But it helps to have a working head. It keeps your mind focused.

Now start to prime the editorial staff – news, features and syndication. Mention you've got something hot but you're going to need time to develop it. A few days later, your editor will be demanding more. At this point, claim that it's even bigger than you thought, and that national security is somehow involved. Over the next few days you:

a) Cultivate a haunted look.

b) Mention to a colleague, in complete confidence, that you're being followed by Special Branch.

This means the entire office will know in a matter of hours.

e) Call the office from home and play some pre-recorded clicks during your conversation. Nothing impresses other journos as much as your phone being tapped.

d) Get a friend to call the office when you're not there. The friend should become extremely agitated, if possible fake the sounds of a struggle followed by a gunshot before hanging up.

e) Forget to submit your expense claims. That will really prove to your editor that you are working on something big.

But you need proof. This you get from:

1. Comments from reputable sources, such as Buckingham Palace.

2. Confirmation from not-quite reputable sources, like UFO watching organisations, preferably in the US since this will discourage most people from doing their own confirmatory checking.

Reputable sources are easy. Spokespeople are notorious for neither confirming nor denying any story that they haven't themselves originated.

This allows you to say:

"Palace sources were keeping a close-mouthed silence last night over the amazing claims that ...."

The crazies in the States will confirm practically anything, and most of them have pretty impressive sounding degrees, hence:

"Noted expert Dr Hiram Kowalski, of NASA (not mentioning that the initials stand for the National Alien Search Association, and that it's headquartered in an abandoned gas station deep in the Arizona desert) confirmed in an exclusive interview (no-one else has spoken to him in years) that ... "

Meanwhile, you've picked up on all the anomalies in the subject's background (everyone has anomalies in their background) and you've fleshed out the story by bringing in MI5, Special Branch, the CIA and a quote from the Archbishop of Canterbury.

Still you haven't done quite enough. You need a show business celebrity, preferably a pop star whom you can convince that the story could be real. It gives you the truth of your fictitious piece – someone famous actually believes it. This presents no problem since most stars will believe anything if it means being associated with Royalty or getting a front page mention.

Now you can rewrite your working head. When all hell breaks out, your excuse is you've only reported what someone actually believes. Note that you're not claiming it, only that someone else is.

Finally you leak part of the story to rival newspapers and wire services. This means your editor will be jumping up and down with frustration at your failure to come up with the story that he's discovered rival newspapers are busily chasing – until you give him the finished piece, some thirty minutes before deadline. This he can't ignore: he knows you've been working on it for some time and, more importantly, he knows other papers are after the same story.

Bingo, you've got your front page splash.

GLOSSARY

Above the fold – A front page story printed in a prime position, because it can be seen while the paper is on the newsagent's counter or in racks.

Splash – The dominant story. Often composed of a headline, two lines and 'turn to page 22'.

By-lines – Published names of journalists in a newspaper who thereby claim credit for a specific item or article (but never blame). A regularly by-lined journalist is often regarded as being at the top of his or her profession, particularly by editors who figure that if they allow a journalist a by-line, they won't have to pay them so much. By-lines are also proudly used by a newspaper when someone famous is writing something for it. Or rather, someone famous is signing his/her name to something that has been written by a staff writer.

Broadsheet – Newspapers that, because of their large page size, are impossible to read on the bus or train. It was once thought that this awkward size was based on some arcane printing requirement, but recent research has proved otherwise. The page size of the *New York Times*, *The Times*, *Figaro*, etc. is based on the smallest newspaper sheet that can successfully wipe up after your dog or cat has been caught short. Broadsheets provide valuable employment for those journalists who are incapable of writing less than three thousand words.

Gutter press – Those newspapers that commit the cardinal sins of being rude/irreverent about people/

institutions that everyone knows should be above criticism (like all union officials, civil servants, politicians and football, rugby and cricket selectors). They tell the general public what it really wants to know, e.g. what else Michael Jackson has had lifted and how much it cost him. This is known as pandering to society's baser instincts and is worth a minimum three million circulation any day.

Quality press – Those newspapers that pride themselves on supporting (or at worst, politely admonishing) people/institutions that everyone knows are above criticism. They tell the general public (who mostly aren't interested anyway) what it really should know. And what its regular readers should think. This is known as responsible journalism. If successful, it leads to declining circulation, newspaper bankruptcy, a peerage for the proprietor and a knighthood for the editor.

Copy – Basic article/news item produced by a journo between drinks or filling out expenses.

Filed copy – Basic article/news item received by a newspaper, invariably late. Once a journo has filed copy, he or she traditionally vanishes until that edition of the newspaper has been printed. This means that they don't have to answer such vital editorial/legal questions as "Are you sure the Pope's Catholic?"

Subbed copy – Basic article/news item after subeditors have worked their magic on it. Or wrecked it completely, depending on your point of view.

Copytasters and takers – The unsung heroes of the subbing world.

Wire services – Agencies that collect news from all over the world and send it on to subscribers. Some newspapers credit the wire service if they use an item. Some pay a bit more so they can re-title it 'From our Special Correspondent'.

Door stepping – Practice of hanging around the home of someone newsworthy in the hope of an interview, a picture or a cup of tea – only to discover that a **buy out** has taken place; i.e. the subject has already signed with another paper and is far away in some plush hotel.

Freebie – Free trip or gift given to a journo (hopefully) in exchange for a favourable, but naturally unbiased, story. Ha, ha.

Design – What distinguishes a newspaper from its rivals, and what most papers don't have.

Layout – Making words and pictures look good when lumped together on a page. Tabloid layouts traditionally begin with a headline and a picture, with words to fit. But one new quality has beaten that: its page layouts begin with the picture on its own, with headlines and copy to follow. The result is terrible, but the picture editor's a happy man.

Cut-and-paste – The way that different stories can be 'hacked' about in order to make them fit the page, or the proprietor's, prejudices.

Up-and-down – Derogatory term for newspapers (particularly tabloids) that look as if they've been designed in vertical columns.

Caxton – Legendary printer who first popularized movable type, thus making redundant whole armies of monks.

New Tech – Producing newspapers using computers which enables 'satellite' printing (different presses fed by wire from a central location); satellite transmission (a newspaper printed simultaneously in different continents), and a host of other electronic tricks.

Word Processor – That which allows you to write, edit, cut and paste all in approximately twice the time it took before.

Kerning – Adjusting the spaces between individual letters in a headline to produce the best effect.

Drop cap – Fancy business with the opening letter of a paragraph.

Screamer – Also known as 'dog-dick': exclamation marks, often used in conjunction with:

Starbursts – Multi-pointed star shapes inside which a word or words have been printed, e.g. FREE; AMAZING; SEXY; ONLY 20p.

WOB – Reversing a headline out of a solid black shape, usually square or rectangular although circles and ovals are gaining in popularity. A useful device for making something look and sound more important than it really is, hence the expression: 'When In Doubt, WOB It Out.'

Strapline/standfirst – Line or so of copy below the headline which encapsulates the whole story. Some believe that all a story needs is a headline, strapline and picture. Not to be confused with panty line, bikini line or party line.

Sign-off – a) figure printed at the end of a piece of copy to show that it's finished; b) the final sentence/paragraph in an article that sums up the entire piece with wit and flair, usually written in near panic to finish the piece before the pubs shut.

Silly season – That time of year when all sorts of really strange and sillier-than-usual stories appear in the press. This usually happens in August, when most journalists and subs are away on holiday, meaning that for once the real world appears in print.

Think piece – A carefully thought out, often elegantly constructed and occasionally well written article commenting on: society, the world in general, the burning issue of the day, the latest hemlines. Few people read think pieces, unless they're about the latest hemlines. Or pornography. Or both. Fewer people understand them. But everyone thinks that think pieces are nice to have around, since there's something traditional reassuring about them. Unlike hemlines.

Press Release – Pungent phrases that the journo can rip-off as his or her own, or more usually, three or four pages of turgid prose that the journalist throws away the day before the editor asks for a piece on that very subject.

Working-head – Device some journos use to remind them what they're supposed to be writing about.

Journalism – Society's defence against the corrupt, the pretentious and the pompous. The fact that journalists are often all three does not change this one little bit.

THE AUTHOR

Nigel Foster blames his childhood love of journalism on vegetables wrapped in copies of the *News of the World*. This resulted in a taste for spinach and interest in sex and scandal that has lasted to this day.

His youth was blighted by school newspapers that never quite came out on time, and a student newspaper that did, but was banned for obscenity. He joined the Army and now claims this was the making of him. The Army denies all responsibility.

He later emigrated to Canada where he learnt to enjoy rye whisky, rare steak and snow. He also came to appreciate a British sense of humour which is why he now lives in London where he writes on a wide variety of subjects, and is available for weddings, bar mitzvahs and funerals.

The second edition of his first best-selling book *The Making of a Royal Marine Commando* is now available. He would like you to buy it since he has two daughters and a Norfolk Crumb Hound to support

He strongly denies that this *Bluffer's Guide* is in any way autobiographical. His friends, colleagues and sometime employers know that it is.

THE BLUFFER'S GUIDES

Available at £1.99 and (new titles* £2.50) each:

Accountancy
Advertising
Antiques
Archaeology
Astrology & Fortune Telling
Ballet
Bird Watching
Bluffing
British Class
Champagne*
The Classics
Computers
Consultancy
Cricket
The European Community
Espionage
Finance
The Flight Deck
Golf
The Green Bluffer's Guide
Japan
Jazz
Journalism
Literature
Management

Marketing
Maths
Modern Art
Motoring
Music
The Occult
Opera
Paris
Philosophy
Photography
P.R.
Public Speaking
Publishing
Racing
Secretaries
Seduction
Sex
Small Business*
Teaching
Theatre
University
Weather Forecasting
Whisky
Wine
World Affairs
